THE LITTLE BOOK OF

HAPPINESS

Parts of this book were first published in 2020 by Trigger, an imprint of Shaw Callaghan Ltd.

This expanded edition published in 2023 by OH! an Imprint of Welbeck Non-Fiction Limited, part of Welbeck Publishing Group. Based in London and Sydney. www.welbeckpublishing.com

Disclaimer:

OH! encourages diversity and different viewpoints. However, all views, thoughts, and opinions expressed in this book are not necessarily representative of Welbeck Publishing Group as an organization. All material in this book is set out in good faith for general guidance; no liability can be accepted for loss or expense incurred in following the information given. In particular, this book is not intended to replace expert medical or phyciatric advice. It is intended for informational purposes only and for your own personal use and guidance. It is not intended to diagnose, treat or act as a substitute for professional medical advice.

ISBN 978-1-80069-344-9

Original compilation: Trigger
Editorial: Victoria Denne
Design: Fusion Graphic Design Ltd
Project manager: Russell Porter
Production: Jess Brisley

A CIP catalogue record for this book is available from the British Library

Printed in China

10 9 8 7 6 5 4 3 2 1

THE LITTLE BOOK OF
HAPPINESS

FOR WHEN LIFE
GETS A LITTLE TOUGH

CONTENTS

INTRODUCTION

Modern life can be filled with so much: from the daily commute, a hectic schedule and cooking an evening meal, to those crucial turning points: quitting your job, moving house, finding love. Between the noise, it can be hard to stop and recognize those all-important moments of joy. *The Little Book of Happiness* offers a little guidance for when the scales of life are tipped, times become turbulent and a moment of reflection is needed. From the minds of some of the world's most well-known figures, learn to find your footing, take a breath and feel happy once more.

CHAPTER

1

HAPPINESS
IS...

Defining happiness is almost
as hard as finding it – but that's
not stopped us trying...

Happiness is when what you think, what you say and what you do are in harmony.

Mahatma Gandhi

Happiness is having a large, loving, caring,
close-knit family in another city.

George Burns

Happiness is a place between
too much and too little.

Finnish proverb

All happiness depends on
courage and work.

Honoré de Balzac

Most of the European words for "**happy**" at first meant "**lucky**". Welsh is an exception, where the word meant "**wise**".

Actions are right in proportion as they tend to promote happiness; wrong as they tend to produce the reverse of happiness. By happiness is intended pleasure and the absence of pain.

John Stuart Mill

Success is getting what you want.
Happiness is wanting what you get.

Dale Carnegie

"

Simplicity makes me happy.

Alicia Keys

"

Happiness consists more
in conveniences of pleasure that occur
every day than in great pieces of good
fortune that happen but seldom.

Benjamin Franklin

It's the Little Things #1

The sound of birds singing

There is no cosmetic for
beauty like happiness.

Lady Blessington

Happiness is not a station you arrive at,
but a manner of travelling.

Margaret Lee Runbeck

Whoever said money doesn't buy
happiness didn't know where to shop.

Blair Waldorf, *Gossip Girl*

Doing what you like is freedom.
Liking what you do is happiness.

Frank Tyger

Real happiness is not of temporary enjoyment, but is so interwoven with the future that it blesses for ever.

James Lendall Basford

True happiness is not attained through self-gratification, but through fidelity to a worthy purpose.

Helen Keller

International Happiness Day
is on 20 March.

Independence is happiness.

Susan B. Anthony

The happiness of life is made up of the little charities of a kiss or smile, a kind look, a heartfelt compliment.

Samuel Taylor Coleridge

It's the Little Things #2

Finding money in your pocket
that you'd forgotten about.

He who lives in harmony with himself lives in harmony with the universe.

Marcus Aurelius

Happiness is not doing fun things.
Happiness is doing meaningful things.

Maxime Lagacé

Happiness is the best makeup.

Drew Barrymore

I don't have to take a trip around
the world or be on a yacht in
the Mediterranean to have happiness.
I can find it in the little things,
like looking out into my backyard
and seeing deer in the fields.

Queen Latifah

My mother is a big believer in being
responsible for your own happiness.
She always talked about finding joy in
small moments ...

... and insisted that we stop and take in the beauty of an ordinary day.

Jennifer Garner

Happiness is a gift and the trick is
not to expect it, but to delight in it
when it comes.

Charles Dickens

It's the Little Things #3

Receiving a compliment
from a stranger

I think everybody should get rich
and famous and do everything they
ever dreamed of so they can see that
it's not the answer.

Jim Carrey

We act as though comfort and luxury were the chief requirements in life, when all we need to make us really happy is something to be enthusiastic about.

Charles Kingsley

Happiness lies in the joy of achievement
and the thrill of creative effort.

Franklin D. Roosevelt

Untranslatable happiness #1

Shinrin-yoko

Japanese, meaning
"forest-bathing"

Happiness can only be achieved by looking inward and learning to enjoy whatever life has ...

... and this requires transforming greed into gratitude.

Henry Fielding

Happiness is nothing more than good
health and a bad memory.

Albert Schweitzer

You might not make it to the top,
but if you are doing what you love,
there is much more happiness there
than being rich or famous.

Tony Hawks

Our greatest happiness does not depend
on the condition of life in which chance
has placed us, but is always the result of a
good conscience, good health, occupation,
and freedom in all just pursuits.

Thomas Jefferson

The habit of being happy enables one
to be freed, or largely freed, from the
domination of outward conditions.

Robert Louis Stevenson

CHAPTER
2

THE PURSUIT OF HAPPINESS

Searching for happiness:
the quest of a lifetime or
the ultimate fallacy?
That's up to you to decide...

The pursuit of happiness is a most
ridiculous phrase: if you pursue
happiness you'll never find it.

Carrie Snow

Happiness is secured through virtue;
it is a good attained by man's own will.

Thomas Aquinas

The greater part of our happiness or misery depends on our dispositions and not on our circumstances. We carry the seeds of the one or the other about with us in our minds wherever we go.

Martha Washington

There is no such thing as the
pursuit of happiness, but there
is the discovery of joy.

Joyce Grenfell

It's the Little Things #4

The first bite
of a meal someone else
has cooked for you

Now and then it's good to pause in our pursuit of happiness and just be happy.

Guillaume Apollinaire

The foolish man seeks happiness in the distance, the wise grows it under his feet.

James Oppenheim

It's a helluva start, being able to recognize what makes you happy.

Lucille Ball

Untranslatable happiness #2

Charmolypi

Greek, meaning
"sweet, joy-making sorrow"

I relate to happiness as an ecstatic moment – something you don't create, you encounter.

Yoko Ono

It is difficult to find happiness within oneself, but it is impossible to find it anywhere else.

Arthur Schopenhauer

To be content means that you realize
you contain what you seek.

Alan Cohen

Be happy with what you have and are,
be generous with both, and you won't
have to hunt for happiness.

William E. Gladstone

According to the World Happiness Report, **Finland** is the world's happiest country, followed by Denmark, Switzerland, Iceland, the Netherlands, Norway and Sweden.

It is the very mark of the spirit of rebellion to crave for happiness in this life.

Henrik Ibsen

Happiness is where we find it, but
very rarely where we seek it.

J. Petit Senn

If someone bases his/her happiness on major events like a great job, huge amounts of money, a flawlessly happy marriage or a trip to Paris, that person isn't going to be happy much of the time ...

... If, on the other hand, happiness depends on a good breakfast, flowers in the yard, a drink or a nap, then we are more likely to live with quite a bit of happiness.

Andy Rooney

Be content with what you have;
rejoice in the way things are. When
you realize there is nothing lacking,
the whole world belongs to you.

Lao Tzu

If you want happiness for an hour – take a nap. If you want happiness for a day – go fishing. If you want happiness for a year – inherit a fortune. If you want happiness for a lifetime – help someone else.

Chinese proverb

All happiness or unhappiness solely
depends upon the quality of the object to
which we are attached by love.

Baruch Spinoza

The talent for being happy is
appreciating and liking what you have,
instead of what you don't have.

Woody Allen

CHAPTER
3

CARPE DIEM!

You've only got one life
to live, after all – so don't waste it:
make it a happy one.

Carpe Diem. Seize the day, boys.
Make your lives extraordinary.

John Keating, *Dead Poets Society* (1989)

Life is not a problem to be solved but a reality to be experienced.

Søren Kierkegaard

The moments of happiness we enjoy take us by surprise. It is not that we seize them, but that they seize us.

Ashley Montagu

It's the Little Things #5

The sight of children laughing

Life moves pretty fast, If you don't
stop and look around once in a while,
you could miss it.

Ferris, *Ferris Bueller's Day Off* (1986)

Happiness, not in another place but this place ... not for another hour, but this hour.

Walt Whitman

Untranslatable happiness #3

Sabsung

Thai, meaning
"being revitalized through
something that livens up
one's life"

Don't waste a minute not being HAPPY.
If one window closes, run to the next
window or break down a door.

Brooke Shields

I, not events, have the power to make me happy or unhappy today. I can choose which it shall be. Yesterday is dead, tomorrow hasn't arrived yet ...

... I have just one day, today, and I'm going to be happy in it.

Groucho Marx

Happiness depends upon ourselves.

Aristotle

Action may not bring happiness but there is no happiness without action.

William James

Don't be afraid of new beginnings.
Don't shy away from new people,
new energy, new surroundings.
Embrace new chances at happiness.

Billy Chapata

The most important thing is to enjoy your life – to be happy – it's all that matters.

Audrey Hepburn

Be happy for this moment.
This moment is your life.

Omar Khayyam

Don't ever underestimate the importance you can have because history has shown us that courage can be contagious and hope can take on a life of its own.

Michelle Obama

Roll with the punches and
enjoy every minute of it.

Meghan Markle, Duchess of Sussex

Spread love everywhere you go. Let no one ever come without leaving happier.

Mother Teresa

CHAPTER
4

WHEN HAPPINESS ELUDES US

Take comfort and inspiration
from these words of
wisdom when happiness is hard
to come by.

Even a happy life cannot be without a measure of darkness, and the word happy would lose its meaning if it were not balanced by sadness ...

... It is far better to take things as they come along with patience and equanimity.

Carl Jung

All life is an experiment. The more experiments you make the better.

Ralph Waldo Emerson

It's the Little Things #6

Eating breakfast in bed

You cannot prevent the birds of sadness
from passing over your head, but you can
prevent their making a nest in your hair.

Chinese proverb

But I know, somehow, that only when it is
dark enough can you see the stars.

Martin Luther King Jr.

In our lives, change is unavoidable,
loss is unavoidable. In the adaptability
and ease with which we experience
change, lies our happiness and freedom.

Buddha

Sometimes we don't find the thing that
will make us happy because we can't give
up the thing that was supposed to.

Robert Brault

You are responsible for your life. You can't keep blaming somebody else for your dysfunction. Life is really about moving on.

Oprah Winfrey

The pain of parting is nothing to the
joy of meeting again.

Charles Dickens

Happiness can be found even in the darkest of times, if one only remembers to turn on the light.

Dumbledore, *Harry Potter and the Prisoner of Azkaban*

It's the Little Things #7

Being the first to step
on fresh snow

With freedom, books, flowers, and the moon, who could not be happy.

Oscar Wilde

Forget not that the earth delights to
feel your bare feet and the winds long
to play with your hair.

Kahil Gibran

"

In every job that must be done,
there is an element of fun.

Mary Poppins *Mary Poppins* (1964)

"

It's been my experience that you can
nearly always enjoy things if you make up
your mind firmly that you will.

L. M. Montgomery

Since you get more joy out of giving
joy to others, you should put a good
deal of thought into the happiness
that you are able to give.

Eleanor Roosevelt

The only thing that will make you happy
is being happy with who you are.

Goldie Hawn

You are your best thing.

Beloved, Toni Morrison

Untranslatable happiness #4

Tarab

Arabic, meaning
"musically induced ecstasy
or enchantment"

When you find out who you are,
you find out what you need.

Mama Odie, *The Princess and the Frog* (2009)

5 Things That Science Says Will Make You Happier

1. Practicing daily gratitude

2. Surrounding yourself with positive people

3. Practicing regular acts of kindness

4. Spending more time with friends and family

5. Investing in experiences, not objects

Source:VeryWellMind.com

I think the saddest people always try
their hardest to make people happy
because they know what it's like to
feel absolutely worthless ...

... and they don't want anyone else
to feel like that.

Robin Williams

"

Optimism is a happiness magnet. If you stay positive, good things and good people will be drawn to you.

Mary Lou Retton

"

If you can laugh, you can get through it.

Jami Gertz

Some cause happiness wherever they go;
others whenever they go.

Oscar Wilde

Remember, you're the one who can
fill the world with sunshine.

Snow White, *Snow White and the Seven Dwarves* (1937)

CHAPTER

5

DON`T WORRY, BE HAPPY

If you find yourself fixating
on everything that's wrong,
you'll never be able to appreciate
what's right – so sit back, relax,
and simply BE.

For every minute you are angry you lose sixty seconds of happiness.

Ralph Waldo Emerson

Man is fond of counting his troubles, but he does not count his joys. If he counted them up as he ought to he would see that every lot has enough happiness provided for it.

Fyodor Dostoevsky

Folks are usually about as happy as they
make their minds up to be.

Abraham Lincoln

Untranslatable happiness #5

Waldeinsamkeit

German, meaning
"the comforting feeling of
being in the forest alone"

Don't forget to tell yourself positive
things daily! You must love yourself
internally to glow externally.

Hannah Bronfman

When you relinquish the desire to control
your future, you can have more happiness.

Nicole Kidman

The most wasted of all days is
one without laughter.

Nicolas Chamfort

The **quokka** is known as "the happiest animal in the world" due to its perpetually smiling face.

Time you enjoy wasting is
not wasted time.

Marthe Troly-Curtin

If you aren't grateful for what you already have, what makes you think you would be happy with more?

Roy T. Bennett

It's the Little Things #8

The feel of getting into a freshly made bed

With mirth and laughter let
old wrinkles come.

William Shakespeare

No matter what you're going through,
there's a light at the end of the tunnel and
it may seem hard to get to it but you can.

Demi Lovato

It's the moments that I stopped just to be, rather than do, that have given me true happiness.

Richard Branson

Untranslatable happiness #6

Sobremesa

Spanish, meaning
"the time spent after
finishing a meal, relaxing
and enjoying the company"

Do not anticipate trouble, or worry
about what may never happen.

Benjamin Franklin

I am content; that is a blessing greater than riches; and he to whom that is given need ask no more.

Henry Fielding

Mr. Happy is the third title in
Roger Hargreaves' *Mr. Men* series,
published in 1971.

The record for the longest time smiling is held by Mariana Costa, who smiled for 2 hours, 2 minutes and 4 seconds.

The happiness of your life depends upon
the quality of your thoughts.

Marcus Aurelius

The more grateful I am, the
more beauty I see.

Mary Davis

The mere sense of living is joy enough.

Emily Dickinson

It's the Little Things #9

Waking up to the smell of fresh
coffee and bread

You're a happy fellow, for you'll
give happiness and joy to many
other people. There is nothing better
or greater than that!

Ludwig van Beethoven

Just think happy thoughts and you'll fly.

Peter Pan, J.M. Barrie

Don't underestimate the value of
Doing Nothing, of just going along,
listening to all the things you can't
hear, and not bothering.

Winnie-the-Pooh

Untranslatable happiness #7

Fjaka

Croatian, meaning
"the sweetness of
doing nothing"

I'd far rather be happy than right any day.

Douglas Adams

You will become way less concerned with what other people think of you when you realize how seldom they do.

Infinite Jest, David Foster Wallace

The first recipe for happiness is: avoid too lengthy meditation on the past.

André Maurois

The secret of health for both mind and body is not to mourn for the past, worry about the future, or anticipate troubles ...

... but to live in the present moment
wisely and earnestly.

Buddha

CHAPTER

6

THE SECRET TO HAPPINESS

Some final words of advice
on the secret to a happy life.

It's part of life to have obstacles.
It's about overcoming obstacles;
that's the key to happiness.

Herbie Hancock

There is only one happiness in this life, to love and be loved.

George Sand (a.k.a. Amantine Lucile Aurore Dupin)

Happiness quite unshared can scarcely
be called happiness; it has no taste.

Charlotte Brontë

Nothing brings me more happiness
than trying to help the most vulnerable
people in society.

Princess Diana

We all want to help one another.
Human beings are like that. We want
to live by each other's happiness,
not by each other's misery.

Charlie Chaplin

Untranslatable happiness #8

Tilfreds

Danish, meaning
"satisfied, at peace"

It's in responsibility that most people find the meaning that sustains them through life. It's not in happiness. It's not in impulsive pleasure.

Jordan Peterson

To be kind to all, to like many and
love a few, to be needed and wanted
by those we love, is certainly the nearest
we can come to happiness.

Mary Stuart

Very little is needed to make a
happy life; it is all within yourself,
in your way of thinking.

Marcus Aurelius

Best Movies About Happiness

Forrest Gump (1994)

Sister Act (1992)

The Sound of Music (1965)

Eat, Pray, Love (2010)

It's a Wonderful Life (1946)

Billy Elliot (2000)

Happy Feet (2006)

Good Will Hunting (1997)

Love Actually (2003)

Little Miss Sunshine (2006)

Source: DevelopGoodHabits.com

My family didn't have a lot of money, and I'm grateful for that. Money is the longest route to happiness.

Evangeline Lilly

It's not possible to experience constant euphoria, but if you're grateful, you can find happiness in everything.

Pharrell Williams

It's the Little Things #10

The warmth of a fire when
it's cold outside

I had the epiphany that laughter was
light, and light was laughter, and that this
was the secret of the universe.

The Goldfinch, Donna Tartt

I must learn to be content with being happier than I deserve.

Jane Austen

Three grand essentials to happiness in this life are something to do, something to love, and something to hope for.

Joseph Addison

The Happiest Jobs on the Planet

1. Engineer
2. Hairdresser/Barber
3. Teacher
4. Nurse
5. Marketers and PR People
6. Medical Practitioner
7. Gardener
8. Scientist
9. Plumber
10. Personal Assistant

Source: TheRichest.com

If you want to be happy, set a goal that
commands your thoughts, liberates your
energy and inspires your hopes.

Andrew Carnegie

Doing what you were born to do ...
that's the way to be happy.

Agnes Martin

It is not how much we have, but how much we enjoy, that makes happiness.

Charles Spurgeon

Untranslatable happiness #9

Desbunar

Portuguese, meaning
"shedding one's inhibitions
while having fun"

The true secret of happiness lies
in taking a genuine interest in all
the details of daily life.

William Morris

Let us be grateful to the people
who make us happy ...

... they are the charming gardeners
who make our souls blossom.

Marcel Proust

There is no happiness like that of
being loved by your fellow creatures,
and feeling that your presence is an
addition to their comfort.

Charlotte Brontë

Happiness depends more on the inward disposition of mind than on outward circumstances.

Benjamin Franklin

My happiness grows in direct
proportion to my acceptance ...

... and in inverse proportion
to my expectations.

Michael J. Fox

Remember that the happiest
people are not those getting
more, but those giving more.

H. Jackson Brown, Jr

Untranslatable happiness #10

Flâner

French, meaning "strolling
leisurely on the streets"

The greatest happiness of life is
the conviction that we are loved;
loved for ourselves, or rather, loved
in spite of ourselves.

Victor Hugo

And now here is my secret, a very simple secret: It is only with the heart that one can see rightly; what is essential is invisible to the eye.

The Little Prince, Antoine de Saint-Exupéry

Stay positive and happy. Work hard and don't give up hope. Be open to criticism and keep learning ...

... Surround yourself with happy, warm and genuine people.

Tena Desae

If you want to be happy, be.

Leo Tolstoy